The Freixenet
Book of Toasts
and Graces

As the producer of the world's favorite
méthode champenoise sparkling wine, Freixenet
wants to make sure that whenever you raise your
glass in a toast, you're not at a loss for words.

So we've completed this booklet to help
you come up with the perfect toast
for any occasion.

If, by chance, you have a favorite toast
we've missed, drop us a line and we'll consider
including it in our next edition.

Cheers!

Write to: Freixenet USA
P.O. Box 1949
Sonoma, California 95476

Méthode Champenoise—CAVA—

Freixenet, a Family Affair

By the time America achieved its independence in 1776, our family had accumulated five hundred years of wine-making experience in Catalonia, Spain.

Today, we're the largest maker of sparkling wine in the world. As you can imagine, it plays a big part in our lives. We still live and work and entertain at the Freixenet Winery, located in a small town near Barcelona.

We put this booklet together to help your family know a little bit more about toasting and our family's lifetime passion—sparkling wine.

How Does the Wine Get All Those Bubbles?

People always ask us how we get so many bubbles in a bottle. We use the traditional French champagne method, where the effervescence is created in each individual bottle. This is called *méthode champenoise*. In Spain, a sparkling wine made this way is called *cava*.

We start making *cava* in the early fall, when the grapes reach a precise balance of natural sugar and acid content. We pick and rush them to the winery, where they are gently pressed. Then yeast is added and the juice goes through its first fermentation.

Next, the winemaker draws upon a lifetime of skill and experience. He fashions a *cuvée*, or blend, for a second fermentation. This happens within the bottle, which is placed in the cool darkness of subterranean caves.

After, say, two years, the trapped CO_2 becomes part of the wine (bubbles), but the yeast needs to be taken out. The bottles are placed in *riddling racks* to be turned and tilted daily until the spent yeast is coaxed into the neck and removed.

Just before corking, we add a bit of wine and sugar to determine the final sweetness of the wine. This is called the *dosage*.

Finally, we rest the bottles one more time before shipment. Sound painstaking? It's the only way we know how to make a sparkling wine as wondrously dry and lively as Freixenet.

When to Serve Sparkling Wine

Sparkling wine used to be served only at very special celebrations. But now folks are enjoying it at all kinds of occasions: parties, brunches, barbecues, before and after special dinners. Fact is, sparkling wine goes with almost any meal—*there's no need to worry about matching white wine or red wine with what food.* One thing hasn't changed, though. Sparkling wine means fun and excitement.

How to Serve Sparkling Wine

To really enjoy sparkling wine, serve it chilled, but don't get carried away. An hour in the refrigerator or thirty minutes in an ice bucket should be perfect.

Hint: Don't chill the glass if you want to get the most flavors and bubble trails. Use well-rinsed and dry, tall flutes or tulip-shaped glasses for longer-lasting bubbles.

Sparkling wine—especially a true *méthode champenoise*—is under great pressure in the bottle, so be extra careful when you open it. Open only chilled wine and never shake the bottle.

Remove the foil and loosen the wire cage that holds the cork. NEVER LOSE HOLD OF THE CORK AFTER YOU LOOSEN THE WIRE CAGE. Now point the bottle away from you—and others. Put a cloth over the cork. Tilt the bottle at a 45 degree angle and slowly twist the bottle, not the cork.

A loud "POP" should only happen in the locker room after the Super Bowl. Impress your guests by easing out the cork so that you only hear a soft "sigh" as the gas escapes. Then, together, appreciate your good taste.

How Much to Serve

There are six glasses of wine in a 750 ml bottle. That should help you plan how much to have on hand. It's also a good idea to have sparkling water or ginger ale for non-drinkers and designated drivers.

Hints for Effective Toasting

1. *Do it in a way that is most comfortable to you. You may remain seated.* Legend has it that it became acceptable to toast without standing in Britain during the reign of Charles II. The king allowed that this would be acceptable after he had risen in response to a toast in his honor while aboard the ship *Royal Charles* and bashed his head into a beam. A similar bashing to King William IV, when he was heir to the throne and toasted George IV while aboard a man-of-war, forever ended the custom of standing toasts in the Royal Navy.

2. *Don't mix toasts with other messages.* During World War II at a banquet given by Marshal Joseph Stalin at the Russian embassy in Teheran, Stalin rose to his feet after Churchill, Roosevelt, and other leaders had been toasted. He grinned and made a quick, impromptu remark in Russian. Judging from the smiles on the faces of the Russians present, it could only be concluded that he had come up with a witty and appropriate toast. As the Americans and British grabbed their

glasses, the interpreter rose to say, "Marshal Stalin says the men's room is on the right."

3. *If you are in some position where you are likely to be called on, it is a good idea to have a few short toasts memorized.* A groom at his own wedding banquet was asked to propose a toast to the bride. Unprepared, he got to his feet, put his hand on the bride's shoulder and said, "Ladies and gentlemen, I . . . I don't know what to say. This thing was forced upon me—"

4. *Check the context of your toast if it is quoted from a known poem or prose work.* Prince Philip of Great Britain was told the story of the man who toasted him at a banquet with two lines from John Dryden:

> A man so various he seemed to be
> Not one but all mankind's epitome.

Philip liked the lines and later looked up the remaining lines of the poem:

> Stiff in opinions, always in the wrong
> Was everything but starts and nothing long;
> But in the course of revolving moon
> Was chemist, fiddler, statesman and buffoon.

5. *Don't get ahead of yourself.* When Queen Louise of Prussia met the conquering Napoleon she drank to him:

"To the health and kindness of Napoleon the

Great. He has taken our states, and soon will return them to us."

Napoleon bowed and replied, "Do not drink it all, Madame."

6. *Make sure that the toast you are delivering is appropriate to the group at hand.* "Bottoms up" would be inappropriate at the beginning of a boat race.

7. *Don't push somebody who is not so inclined to propose a toast. The result may not be the one desired.* There are many examples but a perfect case in point involved Winston Churchill in the 1920s after he had served as First Lord of Admiralty. At a dinner party, someone pestered him for a toast to the traditions of the Royal Navy. "The traditions of the Royal Navy?" was his final response, "I'll give you the traditions of the Royal Navy. Rum, buggery and the lash."

8. *When proposing a toast, make sure you know what you are drinking.* Basic advice, but listen to Rudy Maxa reporting on toasting in the nation's capital in the September 1986 *Washingtonian*: "Then there's the story, perhaps apocryphal, about an American military man toasting his Japanese hosts at a Washington dinner party. Mistaking a finger bowl for a goblet, he finished his remarks and drank deeply from the bowl. Not wishing to offend, fellow guests reached for their own finger bowls and followed suit."

9. *Don't drink with old Saxons.* An old Saxon toasting custom required that a man draw the sharp edge of his knife across his forehead, letting the blood drip into his wine cup and then drinking a health to the woman he loved.

10. *If it's a speech they want, here's an effective outline from Mary Eleanor Roberts:*

Dinner Speech

Three long breaths.
Compliment to the audience.
Funny story.
Outline of what speaker is *not* going to say.
Points that he will touch on later.
Two Bartlett's Familiar Quotations.
Outline of what speaker *is* going to say.
Points that he has not time to touch on now.
Reference to what he said first.
Funny story.
Compliment to the audience.
Ditto to our City, State, and Country.
Applause.
N.B. For an oration, use same formula, repeating each sentence three times in slightly different words.

Toasts
and Toasting

age

A man is only as old as the woman he feels.
—GROUCHO MARX

Do not resist growing old—many are denied the privilege.

Here's a health to the future;
   A sigh for the past;
We can love and remember,
   And hope to the last,
And for all the base lies
   That the almanacs hold
While there's love in the heart,
   We can never grow old.

Long life to you and may you die in your own bed.

May the Lord love us but not call us too soon.

May you enter heaven late.

May you live as long as you want, may you never
want as long as you live.

Only the young die good.

—OLIVER HERFORD

The good die young—here's hoping that you
may live to a ripe old age.

To the old, long life and treasure;
To the young, all health and pleasure.

—BEN JONSON

america

America and England: and may they
never have any division but the
Atlantic between them.

—CHARLES DICKENS

Here's to the memory
Of the man
That raised the corn
That fed the goose
That bore the quill
That made the pen
That wrote the Declaration of Independence.

One flag, one land, one heart, one hand, one nation evermore.
—OLIVER WENDELL HOLMES

Our country, Congress, cash, and courage.

Our country! When right, to be kept right. When wrong, to be put right!
—CARL SCHURZ, *who was doubtlessly responding to a statement by Stephen Decatur (1779–1820) that was a very popular toast for many years and which became a rallying cry for supporters of U.S. government policies during the Vietnam War.*

To America: With all its faults and blemishes, this country gives a man elbowroom to do what is nearest his heart.
—In ERIC HOFFER'S First Things, Last Thing

To our country! Lift your glasses!
To its sun-capped mountain passes,
To its forest, to its streams,
To its memories, its dreams.

anniversaries

Here is to loving, to romance, to us.
May we travel together through time.
We alone count as none, but together we're one,
For our partnership puts love to rhyme.
—*Irish*

Here's to you both—
a beautiful pair,
on the birthday
of your love affair.

Let anniversaries come and let anniversaries
go—but may your happiness continue on
forever.

*Love seems the swiftest, but it is the slowest of
growths. No man or woman really knows what
perfect love is until they have been married a
quarter of a century.*

—MARK TWAIN

May the warmth of our affections survive the
frosts of age.

We've holidays and holy days, and memory days
　　galore;
And when we've toasted every one, I offer just
　　one more.
So let us lift our glasses high, and drink a silent
　　toast—
The day, deep buried in each heart, that each
　　one loves the most.

babies & children

A baby will make love stronger, days shorter, nights longer, bankroll smaller, home happier, clothes shabbier, the past forgotten, and the future worth living for.

A lovely being scarcely formed or molded,
A rose with all its sweetest leaves yet folded.

—LORD BYRON

Grandchildren are gifts of God.
It is God's way . . .
Of compensating us for growing old.

—*Irish*

better times

A speedy calm to the storms of life.

Everybody in life gets the same amount of ice. The rich get it in the summer and the poor in the winter.

—*Words found in the typewriter of
sportswriter Bat Masterson
after he suffered a fatal heart attack.*

If this is a blessing, it is certainly *very* well disguised.

—WINSTON CHURCHILL on his defeat in the 1945 general election, quoted by Richard Nixon in Memoirs of Richard Nixon.

May poverty always be a day's march behind us.

May the sunshine of comfort dispel the clouds of despair.

biblical

A feast is made for laughter, and wine maketh merry.

—Ecclesiastes 10:19

E*at thy bread with joy, and drink thy wine with a merry heart.*

—Ecclesiastes 9:7

W*ine maketh glad the heart of man.*

—Psalms 104:15

Wine was created from the beginning to make men joyful, and not to make men drunk. Wine drunk with moderation is the joy of the soul and the heart.

—*Ecclesiastes* 31:35–36

birthdays

Here's to you! No matter how old you are, you don't look it!

May you live to be a hundred years with one extra year to repent.

—*Irish*

To wish you joy on your birthday
And all the whole year through,
For all the best that life can hold
Is none too good for you.

To your birthday, glass held high,
Glad it's you that's older—not I.

champagne

Here's champagne to your real friends and real pain to your sham friends.

Here's to champagne, the drink divine,
That makes us forget all our troubles;
It's made of a dollar's worth of wine
And three dollars' worth of bubbles.*

*Some take their gold
In minted mold,
And some in harps hereafter,
But give me mine
In bubbles fine
And keep the change in laughter.*

—OLIVER HERFORD

christmas

A Christmas wish—
May you never forget
what is worth remembering
or remember
what is best forgotten.

—*Irish*

At Christmas play and make good cheer
For Christmas comes but once a year.

—THOMAS TUSSER

*This is the original version of this toast, at least ninety
years old; so you may want to inflate the dollar amounts to
update it.

"**B**lessed is the season which engages the whole world in a conspiracy of love."

—HAMILTON WRIGHT MABIE

Here's to the holly with its bright red berry.
Here's to Christmas, let's make it merry.

Here's to the day of good will, cold weather, and warm hearts!

Here's to us all!
God bless us every one!

—*Tiny Tim's toast, from*
A Christmas Carol *by* CHARLES DICKENS

Here's wishing you more happiness
Than all my words can tell,
Not just alone for Christmas
But for all the year as well.

***H**olly and ivy hanging up*
And something wet in every cup.

—*Irish*

May you be the first house in the parish to welcome St. Nicholas.

—*Irish*

21

May your corn stand high as yourself, your fields grow bigger with rain, and the mare know its own way home on Christmas night.

—Irish

May your sheep all have lambs but not on Christmas night.

—Irish

Peace and plenty for many a Christmas to come.

—Irish

Then let us be merry and taste the good cheer, And remember old Christmas comes but once a year.

—From an old Christmas carol

cities & towns

Boston

And this is good old Boston,
The home of the bean and the cod,
Where the Lowells talk to the Cabots,
And the Cabots talk only to God.

—DR. JOHN C. BOSSIDY,
at alumni dinner of Holy Cross College

Chicago

Chicago sounds rough to the maker of verse;
One comfort we have—Cincinnati sounds worse.
> —OLIVER WENDELL HOLMES

Hollywood

Here's to Hollywood—
A place where people from Iowa
Mistake each other for movie stars.
> —FRED ALLEN

"Our Town"

Here's to our town—a place where people
spend money they haven't earned to buy
things they don't need to impress people they
don't like.

I would rather be with the people of this town than
with the finest people in the world.
> —*Toast proposed by the mayor to his*
> *firefighters in the movie* Roxanne

Washington, D.C.

First in war, first in peace, and last in the American
League.
> —*This, of course, an allusion to the*
> *long-suffering Washington Senators baseball team*

fishing

A bad day of fishing is still better than a good day at work.

—*Bumper sticker*

Here's to Fishing—a grand delusion enthusiastically promoted by glorious liars in old clothes.

—DON MARQUIS

Here's to our fisherman bold,
Here's to the fish he caught;
Here's to the one that got away,
And here's to the one he bought.

There are more fish taken out of a stream than ever were in it.

—OLIVER HERFORD

food

A full belly, a heavy purse, and a light heart.

Eat well's drink well's brother.

—*Old Scottish proverb*

Let the dogs wait a long time.

—*Irish wish for a lengthy and ample dinner*

May you always have red-eye gravy with your ham, hush puppies with your catfish, and the good sense not to argue with your wife.

—*Toast from Tennessee, quoted by Timothy Noah in the* New Republic

friendship

Absent friends—though out of sight we recognize them with our glasses.

Friendship: May differences of opinion cement it.

Here's to a friend. He knows you well and likes you just the same.

Here's to beefsteak when you're hungry,
Whiskey when you are dry,
Greenbacks when you are busted,
And Heaven when you die!

Here's to Eternity—may we spend it in as good company as this night finds us.

Here's to our friends . . . and the strength to put up with them.
—*Line used in ads for the movie* The Four Seasons

May the friends of our youth be the companions of our old age.

May we have more and more friends, and need them less and less!

The Lord gives our relatives,
Thank God we can choose our friends.

To our best friends, who know the worst about us but refuse to believe it.

To the spirit of Christmases yet to come.
—World War II toast

Be glad of life!
Because it gives you the chance to love and work,
To play and to look up at the stars.
—HENRY VAN DYKE

Blue skies and green lights.

Good company, good wine, good welcome make good people.
—SHAKESPEARE

26

*Here's to becoming top banana without losing touch
with the bunch.*
—BILL COPELAND *in the* Sarasota Journal

Here's to old Massachusetts
The home of the sacred cod
Where the Adamses vote for Douglas
And the Cabots walk with God.
*—Given at the Twenty-fifth Anniversary
Dinner of the Harvard class of 1880*

Here's to us that are here, to you that are there,
and the rest of us everywhere.
—RUDYARD KIPLING

It is best to rise from life as from the banquet,
neither thirsty nor drunken.
—ARISTOTLE

Love to one, friendship to many, and good will to all.

Make every day a masterpiece.

May life last as long as it is worth wearing.

Make the most of life when you may,
Life is short and wears away!
—WILLIAM OLDYS

May the work that you have
Be the play that you love!

—E. GERBERDING

May those who deceive us be always deceived.

May our feast days be many and our fast days
be few.

—MARY L. BOOTH

May *you have warmth in your igloo, oil in your lamp,
and peace in your heart.*

—*Eskimo toast*

May we all live in pleasure and die out of debt.

May we be happy and our enemies know it.

May we live respected and die regretted.

May we breakfast with Health, dine with
Friendship, crack a bottle with Mirth, and sup
with the goddess Contentment.

May we live to learn well,
And learn to live well.

May we never do worse.

May we never feel want, nor ever want feeling.

May we be merry and lack nothing.
—SHAKESPEARE

May you live all the days of your life.
—JONATHAN SWIFT

May you live as long as you want to and want to as long as you live.

May your life be as beautiful as a summer day with just enough clouds to make you appreciate the sunshine.
—Found inscribed in a book and dated 1882

Sex: The pleasure is momentary; the expense is exorbitant; the position ridiculous.
—G. K. CHESTERTON

S*o live that when you come to die, even the undertaker will feel sorry for you.*
—MARK TWAIN

Success to the lover, honor to the brave,
Health to the sick, and freedom to the slave.

'Tis hard to tell which is best,
Music, Food, Drink, or Rest.

To the old, long life and treasure;
To the young, all health and pleasure;
   To the fair, their face,
   With eternal grace;
And the rest, to be loved at leisure.

—BEN JONSON

To California. Where Earth is here so kind that
just tickle her with a hoe and she laughs with a
harvest.

—ERNEST JARROLD

To the good old days . . . we weren't
so good, 'cause we weren't so old!

Be present at our table, Lord.
Be here and everywhere adored.
These mercies bless, and grant that we
May feast in Paradise with Thee.

—JOHN CENNICK, 1741

Bless, O Lord, this food to our use, and us to
Thy service, and make us ever needful of the
needs of others, in Jesus' name, Amen.

—*Traditional Protestant grace*

Bless us, O Lord, and these Thy gifts which we
have received out of Thy bounty, through Christ
Our Lord. Amen.

—*Traditional Catholic grace*

Come, Lord Jesus, Be our Guest, and let Thy
gifts to us be blessed. Amen.

For the air we breathe,
and the water we drink,
For a soul and a mind
with which to think,
For food that comes
from fertile sod,
For these, and many things
I'm thankful to my God.

—*Thanksgiving grace written by comedian
Danny Thomas when he was in the sixth grade.*

For what we are about to receive, the Lord make
us truly thankful, for Christ's sake. Amen.

—*Old English classic which is probably the
best known of all Christian English-language graces.*

G*od bless the master of this house,*
God bless the mistress too;
And all the little children
Who round the table go.

—*Traditional British grace*

God is great, God is good,
We will thank Him for this food.
By his hand must all be fed
Thanks be to God for our daily bread.
—Traditional children's grace

Good bread, good meat
Good God, let's eat!

Heavenly father bless us,
And keep us all alive:
There's ten of us for dinner
And not enough for five.

Lift up your hands toward the sanctuary and
    bless the Lord.
Blessed art Thou, O Lord our God, King of the
    Universe,
who brings forth bread from the earth. Amen.
—Traditional Jewish thanksgiving before meals

May the good Lord take a liking to you—but not
too soon!

May our house always be too small to hold all our friends.

—MYRTLE REED

See, your guests approach:
Address yourself to entertain them sprightly,
And let's be red with mirth.
> —SHAKESPEARE, Winter's Tale, *Act IV*

The ornament of a house is the guests who
frequent it.

health

*Early to rise and early to bed
makes a male healthy and wealthy
and dead.*
> —JAMES THURBER

Here's a health to every one;
Peace on earth, and heaven won.

Here's to your health! You make age curious,
Time furious, and all of us envious.

The best doctors in the world are Doctor Diet,
Doctor Quiet, and Dr. Merryman.
> —JONATHAN SWIFT

To your good health, old friend,
may you live for a thousand years,
and I be there to count them.
> —ROBERT SMITH SURTEES

home

God bless our mortgaged home.

Here's to home, the place where we are treated best, and grumble the most.

—From an old postcard

hosts & hostesses

A toast to our host
   And a song from the short and tall of us,
May he live to be
   The guest of all of us!

Here's to our hostess, considerate and sweet;
Her wit is endless, but when do we eat?

May the roof above us never fall in, and may we friends gathered below never fall out.

—Irish

To our host,
An excellent man;
For is not a man
Fairly judged by the
Company he keeps?

To the sun that warmed the vineyard,
   To the juice that turned to wine,
To the host that cracked the bottle,
   And made it yours and mine.

To our hostess! She's a gem. We love her, God
   bless her.
And the devil take her husband.

To our host: The rapturous, wild, and ineffable
pleasure of drinking at somebody else's expense.
                    —HENRY SAMBROOKE LEIGH, 1870

What's a table richly spread
Without a woman at its head?

husbands

Here's to the man who loves his wife,
   And loves his wife alone.
For many a man loves another man's wife,
   When he ought to be loving his own.

May your life be long and sunny
And your husband fat and funny.

> When the husband drinks to the wife, all would
> be well; when the wife drinks to the husband, all is.
> —*Old English proverb*

international

*An assembly of short toasts or, as they have been called,
cheers to get you through a United Nations reception.
Their English equivalents are along the lines of Cheers,
To your health, and Bottoms up.*

Albanian: Gëzuar.
Arabian: Bismillah. Fi schettak.
Armenian: Genatzt
Austrian: Prosit
Belgian: Op uw gezonheid.
Brazilian: Saúde. Viva.
Chinese: Nien Nien nu e. Kong Chien. Kan bei.
    Yum sen. Wen lie.
Czechoslovakian: Na Zdravi. Nazdar.
Danish: Skål
Dutch: Proost. Geluch.
Egyptian: Fee sihetak.
Esperanto: Je zia sano.
Estonian: Tervist.
Finnish: Kippis. Maljanne.
French: A votre santé. Santé.
German: Prosit. Auf ihr wohl.
Greek: Eis Igian.
Greenlandic: Kasûgta.

Hawaiian: Okole maluna. Hauoli maoli oe. Meli
  kalikama.
Hungarian: Kedves egeszsegere.
Icelandic: Santanka nu.
Indian: Jaikind. Aanand.
Indonesian: Selamat.
Iranian: Besalmati. Shemoh.
Italian: A la salute. Salute. Cin cin.
Japanese: Kampai. Banzai.
Korean: Kong gang ul wi ha yo.
Lithuanian: I sveikas.
Malayan: Slamat minum.
Mexican: Salud.
Moroccan: Saha wa'afiab.
New Zealand: Kia ora
Norwegian: Skål.
Pakistani: Sanda bashi.
Philippine Mabuhay.
Polish: Na zdrowie. Vivat.
Portuguese: A sua saúde.
Romanian: Noroc. Pentru sanatatea dunneavoastra.
Russian: Na zdorovia.
Spanish: Salud. Salud, amor y pesetas y el tiempo
  para gustarlos! (Health, love, and money and
  the time to enjoy them!)
Swedish: Skål.
Thai: Sawasdi.
Turkish: Şerefe.
Ukrainian: Boovatje zdorovi.
Welsh: Iechyd da.
Yugoslavia: Zivio.
Zulu: Oogy wawa.

irish

May you have warm words on a cold evening,
A full moon on a dark night,
And the road downhill all the way to your door.

May the road rise to meet you.
May the wind be always at your back,
the sun shine warm upon your face,
the rain fall soft upon your fields,
and until we meet again
may God hold you in the hollow of His hand.

May the rocks in your field turn to gold.

May the saints protect you,
And sorrow neglect you,
And bad luck to the one
That doesn't respect you.

May the sun shine warm upon your face and the
rains fall soft upon your fields.

May you have the hindsight to know where
you've been, the foresight to know where you're
going, and the insight to know when you're
going too far.

May you look back on the past with as much pleasure as you look forward to the future.

May you never make an enemy
when you could make a friend
unless you meet a fox among your chickens.

May your fire be as warm as the weather is cold.

May your fire never go out.

The prime Jewish toast is the Hebrew L'chayim, *which means "to life," or "to your health."* Mazel tov *is also used as a toast. Leo Rosten explains which to use when in his* Joys of Yiddish: *"Some innocents confuse* L'chayim *with* mazel tov, *using one when the other would be appropriate. There is no reason to err.* L'chayim *is used whenever one would say 'Your health,' 'Cheers!' or (I shudder to say) 'Here's mud in your eye.'* Mazel tov! *is used as 'Congratulations.'"*

Drink and be merry, for our time on earth is short, and death lasts forever.

Drink, for you know not
    When you came, nor why,
Drink, for you know not why
    You go, nor whence.
—OMAR KHAYYÁM

Drink with impunity—
Or anyone who happens to invite you!
—ARTEMUS WARD

I drink when I have occasion and sometimes
when I have no occasion.
—MIGUEL DE CERVANTES

love

Because I love you truly,
Because you love me, too,
My very greatest happiness
Is sharing life with you.

Come in the evening, or come in the morning,
Come when you are looked for, or come without
    warning,
A thousand welcomes you will find here before you,
And the oftener you come here the more I'll adore you.
—Irish

40

Drink to me only with thine eyes,
  And I will pledge with mine;
Or leave a kiss but in the cup,
  And I'll not look for wine.

—BEN JONSON, "To Celia"

Here's to love and unity,
Dark corners and opportunity.

Here's to Love, that begins with a fever and ends
with a yawn.

*H*ere's to one and only one,
  And may that one be he
Who loves but one and only one,
  And may that one be me.

Here's to the land we love and the love we
land.

Here's to the prettiest, here's to the wittiest,
Here's to the truest of all who are true,
Here's to the neatest one, here's to the sweetest
  one,
Here's to them all in one—here's to you.

41

Here's to you,
May you live as long as you want to,
May you want to as long as you live.

Here's to you who halves my sorrows and
doubles my joys.

I have known many,
    liked quite a few,
Loved one—
    Here's to you!

I love you more than yesterday, less than
tomorrow.

Love doesn't make the world go 'round. Love is
what makes the ride worthwhile.
—FRANKLIN P. JONES

Love is what you've been through with
somebody.
—JAMES THURBER

May those now love
Who never loved before.
May those who've loved
Now love the more.

May we kiss those we please
And please those we kiss.

May we love as long as we live, and live as long as
we love.

Say it with flowers
    Say it with eats,
Say it with kisses,
    Say it with sweets,
Say it with jewelry,
    Say it with drink,
But always be careful
    Not to say it with ink.

Thou hast no faults, or I no faults can spy;
Thou art all beauty, or all blindness I.

To every lovely lady bright,
I wish a gallant faithful knight;
To every faithful lover, too,
I wish a trusting lady true.

—SIR WALTER SCOTT

The love you give away is the only love you keep.

—ELBERT HUBBARD

luck

As you slide down the banister of life
May the splinters never face the wrong way.

Everything of fortune but her instability.

May the chicken never be hatched that will
scratch on your grave.

military

A stout ship, a clear sea, and a far-off coast in
stormy weather.
> —*Navy*

To our women, our horses, and the men who
ride them.
> —*Calvary toast, World War I, from the French*

To the confounding of our enemies.
> —*Toast favored and made popular by Dean Acheson*

Gold ships, fair winds, and brave seamen.
> —*Navy*

Grog, grub, and glory.

—*Navy*

Here's to the ships of our navy
And the ladies of our land;
May the first be ever well rigged,
And the latter ever well manned.

—*Navy*

May no son of the ocean be devoured by his mother.

—*Navy*

Put your trust in God, boys, and keep your powder dry.

—COLONEL BLACKER

The three generals in peace: General Peace, General Plenty, and General Satisfaction.

—*Army*

To long lives and short wars!
—COLONEL POTTER, *"M*A*S*H"
episode, February 4, 1980*

True hearts and sound bottoms.

—*Navy*

new year's

Be at war with your voices, at peace with your neighbors, and let every new year find you a better man.

—BENJAMIN FRANKLIN

Here's to the bright New Year
   And a fond farewell to the old;
Here's to the things that are yet to come
   And to the memories that we hold.

In the New Year, may your right hand always be stretched out in friendship, but never in want.

—*Irish*

In the year ahead,
May we treat our friends with kindness
and our enemies with generosity.

Let us resolve to do the best we can with what we've got.

—WILLIAM FEATHER

May your nets be always full—
your pockets never empty.
May your horse not cast a shoe
nor the devil look at you
in the coming year.

—*Irish*

Should auld acquaintance be forgot,
    And never brought to min',
Should auld acquaintance be forgot
    And days of auld lang syne.
For auld lang syne, my dear,
    For auld lang syne,
We'll tak' a cup o' kindness yet,
    For auld lang syne.

And here's a hand, my trusty fierce,
    And gie's a hand o' thine,
And we'll tak' a right guid willie-waught,
    For auld lang syne.
For auld lang syne, my dear,
    For auld lang syne,
We'll tak' a cup o' kindness yet,
    For auld lang syne.

And surely ye'll be your pint stowpt,
    And surely I'll be mine,
And we'll tak' a cup o' kindness yet,
    For auld lang syne,
For auld lang syne, my dear,
    For auld lang syne,
We'll tak' a cup o' kindness yet,
    For auld lang syne.

—ROBERT BURNS

parents

Father. May the love and respect we express toward him make up, at least in part, for the worry and care we have visited upon him.

Here's to the happiest hours of my life—
Spent in the arms of another man's wife;
My mother!

To Life. The first half is ruined by our parents and the second half by our children.

To Mother and Dad on their wedding anniversary:
    We never know the love of our parents
    for us till we have become parents.
                                        —HENRY WARD BEECHER

parting

Happy are we met, happy have we been,
Happy may we part, and happy meet again.

Here's to good-byes—that they never be spoken!
Here's to friendships—may they never be broken!

May we always part with regret and meet again with pleasure.

past, present & future

May we always look forward with pleasure, and backward with regret.

The have-beens, the are-nows—and the may-bes!

scottish

A guid New Year to yin and a'
   And mony may you see,
And may the mouse ne'er run out o'
   Your girnel wi' a tear in its 'e.

May the best ye've ever seen
Be the worst ye'll ever see.

May the winds o' adversity ne'er blaw open our door.

Fair thought and happy hours attend on you.
—The Merchant of Venice, *Act III*

Frame your mind to mirth and merriment,
Which bars a thousand harms and lengthens life.
—The Taming of the Shrew, *Act II*

Love sought is good, but given unsought is better.
—Twelfth Night, *Act III*

The best of happiness, honor, and fortunes keep with you.
—Timon of Athens, *Act I*

They do not love that do not show their love.
—The Two Gentlemen of Verona, *Act I*

Here's looking at you, though heaven knows it's an effort.

Here's to a clear conscience—or a poor memory.

The Graduate

A *toast to the Graduate—in a class by him/herself.*

Imperfect Love

Marriage is a lot like the army, everyone complains, but you'd be surprised at the large number that reenlist.

—*Actor* JAMES GARNER

'Tis better to have loved and lost,
Then to marry and be bossed.

Introductory

Here's *mud in your eyes—while I look*
Over your beautiful sweetheart!

On the Trail

A health to the man on the trail tonight;
may his grub hold out; may his dogs keep their
  legs;
may his matches never misfire.

—JACK LONDON

Religion

To Church: The first time one goes he has water thrown on him, the second time he has rice thrown on him, the third time he has dirt thrown on him.

Balloonist

THE BALLOONIST'S PRAYER

May the wind welcome you with softness,
May the sun bless you with his warm hands,
May you fly so high and so well, God joins you in
    laughter,
And may He always set you gently back again
Into the loving arms of Mother Earth.

> —*Since the eighteenth century, champagne has been the
> balloonists' traditional safe-landing celebration
> and, at times, liquid appeasement for angry
> farmers (who thought the original balloonists
> in their fiery contraptions were devils).*

The Cowboy

Here's to luck, and hoping God will take a likin' to us!

> —*Cowboy, Dakota Territory, circa 1880*

Creditors

Here's to our creditors—may they be
Endowed with three virtues:
Faith, Hope, and Charity!

Doctors

Unto our doctors let us drink,
Who cure our chills and ills,
No matter what we really think
About their pills and bills.

—PHILIP MCALLISTER

When Judgment Day arrives and all
The doctors answer for their sins,
O' think of what they'll get who bring
The howling triplets and the twins.

Farmers

Fat cattle, green fields, and many a bushel in
your barn.

—Irish

To Farmers—founders of civilization.

—DANIEL WEBSTER

Lawyers

The glorious uncertainty of the law.

—First found in Macklin's Loveala Mode *(1759).*
Ever since, it has been used
as a toast at legal dinners.

The law: It has honored us; may we honor it.

—DANIEL WEBSTER

The lawyer—a learned gentleman, who rescues your estate from your enemies, and keeps it himself.

To Lawyers: You cannot live without the lawyers, and certainly you cannot die with them.

—JOSEPH H. CHOATE

Novice

Here's to learning the ropes without coming unraveled.

Psychiatrist

Here's to my psychiatrist.
He finds you cracked and leaves you broke.

Toastmaster

A toastmaster is a person who eats a meal he doesn't want so he can get up and tell a lot of stories he doesn't remember to people who've already heard them.

—GEORGE JESSEL

We'll bless our toastmaster,
Wherever he may roam,
If he'll only cut the speeches short
And let us all go home.

The Virgin

Here's to _____
For her, life held no terrors
Born a virgin, died a virgin
No hits, no runs, no errors.

Writers

Authors are judged by strange, capricious rules,
The great ones are thought mad, the small ones
fools.

Writing is a dog's life, but the only life worth
living.

—GUSTAVE FLAUBERT

Bacchus has drowned more men than Neptune.

If you drink like a fish,
Drink what a fish drinks.

Our drink shall be water, bring, sparkling with
  glee
The gift of our God, and the drink of the free.

thanksgiving

Bless, O Lord,
These delectable vittles,
May they add to the glory
And not to our middle.

*—*YVONNE WRIGHT *quoted as a*
"Thanksgiving Prayer" in the 1986
Reader's Digest, *Calendar*

Here's to the blessings of the year,
Here's to the friends we hold so dear,
To peace on earth, both far and near.

Here's to the good old turkey
The bird that comes each fall
And with his sweet persuasive meat
Makes gobblers of us all.

O Thou who has given us so much, mercifully
grant us one thing more—a grateful heart.

*—*GEORGE HERBERT

weddings

A Second Marriage: To the triumph of hope
over experience.

*—*SAMUEL JOHNSON, *1770*

A toast to love and laughter and happily ever after.

Down the hatch, to a striking match!

Grow old with me!
The best is yet to be,
The last of life,
For which, the first is made.

—ROBERT BROWNING

Here's to my mother-in-law's daughter,
　　Here's to her father-in-law's son;
And here's to the vows we've just taken,
　　And the life we've just begun.

Here's to the groom with bride so fair,
And here's to the bride with groom so rare!

Here's to the happy man: All the world loves a lover.

—RALPH WALDO EMERSON

Here's to the husband—and here's to the wife;
May they remain lovers for life.

It is written:
"When children find true love,
parents find true joy."
Here's to your joy and ours,
from this day forward

—Parents' toast

Let us toast the health of the bride;
    Let us toast the health of the groom,
Let us toast the person that tied;
    Let us toast every guest in the room.

Look down you gods,
And on this couple drop a blessed crown.

—SHAKESPEARE

Love, be true to her; Life, be dear to her;
Health, stay close to her; Joy, draw near to her;
Fortune, find what you can do for her,
Search your treasure-house through and through
    for her,
Follow her footsteps the wide world over—
And keep her husband always her lover.

—ANNA LEWIS, *"To the Bride"*

*Marriage is a wonderful institution, but who wants to
live in an institution.*

—GROUCHO MARX

May their joys be as bright as the morning, and their sorrows but shadows that fade in the sunlight of love.

May their joys be as deep as the ocean
And their misfortunes as light as the foam.

May you grow old on one pillow.

—Armenian

May your love be as endless as your wedding rings.

May your wedding days be few and your anniversaries many.

May you have enough happiness to keep you sweet; enough trials to keep you strong; enough sorrow to keep you human; enough hope to keep you happy; enough failure to keep you humble; enough success to keep you eager; enough friends to give you comfort; enough faith and courage in yourself, your business, and your country to banish depression; enough wealth to meet your needs; enough determination to make each day a better day than yesterday.

Never above you. Never below you. Always beside you.
—WALTER WINCHELL

There is nothing nobler or more admirable
than when two people who see eye to eye keep
house as man and wife, confounding their
enemies and delighting their friends.
—HOMER, Odyssey, *ninth century* B.C.

To my wife,
My bride and joy.

To the newlyweds: May "for better or worse" be
far better than worse.

You don't marry one person; you marry three—
the person you think they are, the person they
are, and the person they are going to become as
the result of being married to you.
—RICHARD NEEDHAM, You and All the
Rest, *edited by Jean Shagbaum
(M. Sutkiewicz, Toronto) quoted in*
Reader's Digest, *December 1983*

You only get married for the second time once.
—GARRISON KEILLOR, *quoted in* Forbes,
November 2, 1987

Wedlock's like wine—not properly judged of till
the second glass.
—ERNEST JARROLD

wine

A bottle of good wine, like a good act, shines
ever in the retrospect.

—ROBERT LOUIS STEVENSON, *in*
"The Silverado Squatters"

A warm toast.
Good company.
A fine wine.
May you enjoy all three.

Clean glasses and old corks.

Here's to the man
Who owns the land
That bears the grapes
That makes the wine
That tastes as good
As this does.

Wine, wit, and wisdom.
Wine enough to sharpen wit,
Wit enough to give zest to wine,
Wisdom enough to "shut down" at the right
    time.

When wine enlivens the heart
May friendship surround the table.

Wine and women—May we always have a taste for both.

*W*ine improves with age—I like it more the older I get.

wives

A good wife and health
Are a man's best wealth.

To our wives and sweethearts. May they never meet!

A health to our widows. If they ever marry again may they do as well!

woman & women

Here's looking at you, dear!
Though I should pour a sea of wine,
My eyes would thirst for more.

Here's to God's first thought, "Man"!
Here's to God's second thought, "Woman"!
Second thoughts are always best,
So here's to Woman!

I have never studied the art of paying compliments to women, but I must say that if all that has been said by orators and poets since the creation of the world in praise of women were applied to the women of America, it would not do them justice. God bless the women of America.

—ABRAHAM LINCOLN

To the ladies, God bless them,
May nothing distress them.

'Tween woman and wine a man's lot is to smart,
For wine makes his head ache, and woman his heart.

W*hat, sir, would the people of the earth be without woman? They would be scarce, sir, almighty scarce.*

—MARK TWAIN

The Freixenet Sparkling Wines

Freixenet produces sparkling wine in different styles for different tastes. All of them are made in the traditional champagne method called *méthode champenoise.*

Cordon Negro Brut. This is the world's favorite *méthode champenoise* sparkling wine. It comes in the striking black-frosted bottle. "Brut" means that it's very, very dry. Appropriate for any occasion.

Cordon Negro Extra Dry. This new sparkler is made from the same grapes and fermented in the black bottle the same two years as Cordon Negro Brut. Its slightly higher *dosage* gives it a fuller, slightly fruitier taste.

Carta Nevada Brut and Carta Nevada Semi-Seco. You can recognize Carta Nevada by its distinctive gold bottle and gold label. Carta Nevada has a rich, full taste that makes a perfect wine to serve with flavorful meals or as a mixer for champagne cocktails. The Brut is dry, the Semi-Seco a touch sweeter.

Brut Nature. This is our imperial *cuvée.* It's delicate, bone dry, and many say our best. Brut Nature is a *cuvée* made of reserve wines from those years when a "vintage" is proclaimed.

Brut Rosé. Our new prestige *cuvée.* This *méthode champenoise* sparkler has a taste that's crisp and dry yet fruity. It balances the fruitiness of a good white zin with the elegance and sophistication of an expensive, hard-to-get rosé champagne.

FERMENTED IN THE BOTTLE. MÉTHODE CHAMPENOISE AGED IN THE CAVE.